The Blair Centre:
a question of command and control?

a political commentary by
Peter Hennessy

Public Management Foundation

February 1999

Peter Hennessy is Professor of Contemporary History at Queen Mary and Westfield College, University of London, and Visiting Professor of Government at the University of Strathclyde. His book, *Prime Minister: The Office and its Holders Since 1945*, will be published by Penguin in 2000. This paper was delivered to the Public Management Foundation on 20 October 1998, as one of the Foundation's series of seminars on topical issues affecting the management and delivery of public services.

165 Gray's Inn Road, London, WC1X 8UE
tel: 0171 278 1712; fax 0171 713 1515
email: pmf@pmfoundation.org.uk
web site: www.pmfoundation.org.uk

Preface

The Public Management Foundation is pleased to publish this paper, which Professor Hennessy presented at a seminar organised by the Foundation in October 1998. The meeting was the first in a series of seminars on topical issues for managers, policy makers and politicians concerned with public services. Other seminars in the Autumn series were given by Andrew Slaughter, Mayor of Hammersmith and Fulham, on Innovation in Local Authority Governance and Tony Travers, Director of the Greater London Group at the London School of Economics on The Future of Public Services Regulation.

The speakers' opinions are, of course, their own and do not necessarily represent the views of the Public Management Foundation.

Jane Steele
Principal Research Fellow
Public Management Foundation

The Blair Centre: a question of command and control?

Since the days running up to the 1997 general election I have been attempting what is, for me, something new. Rather like a slightly battered reconnaissance aircraft, I have been trying to photograph this government in flight. Not all of it; that would be impossible. But that section made up of what Tony Blair calls 'the three principal parts of the centre'[1] the Prime Minister's Office, the Cabinet Office and the Treasury – the top end of the government food-chain, as one might describe it. This task is a little difficult, even in the relatively open climate in which Whitehall watchers can now operate. 'Political and Personal Sensitivity' remains, the intelligence and security worlds apart, the highest form of secrecy classification *de facto*.

It's a trifle tricky, too, in professional terms. Contemporary historians are tasked to provide the second rough draft of history (the better end of current affairs journalism serving up the first). And it is the task of political scientists to place pattern on chaos. But attempting to do this a mere 18 months into the life of an administration can be just a bit premature and vulnerable to a rapid overtaking by events. Candour and a touch of the tentative are required, therefore.

May I begin with a quick summary of the two photo-reconnaissance reports I have published since Blair took office? I must, in all honesty, rewind the camera to a few weeks before the 1997 poll. Come with me to an attic room not far from the House of Commons, to a small breakfast meeting of top private sector people and senior civil servants. I was in the chair and the guest speaker was a member of Tony Blair's innermost circle, a position he retains to this day. Conversation turned to the style of government his man would deploy from No.10, the electorate willing. 'You may see,' he said, 'a change from a feudal system of barons to a more Napoleonic system.'[2] Immediately, the senior

Whitehall figures present switched their radars on to full beam. The word quickly got around. They had been warned.

This, rather than anything Blair said publicly about people having 'to know that we will run the centre and govern from the centre'[3], is the phrase that has so far given the Blair premiership its *leitmotif*. Michael White's recent BBC Radio 4 programme in the *Matrix of Power* series quoted the same chap using the same metaphor 18 months on, though he seems now – to mix the metaphor a bit – to regard the Secretary of the Cabinet, Sir Richard Wilson, as the Prime Minister's 'Chief Whip in Whitehall'.[4] The Napoleonic/feudal distinction already looks set fair to echo down the decades in a thousand undergraduate essays on the perpetual tension between the power of the Prime Minister and the requirements of Cabinet government, alongside Margaret Thatcher's assertion to Kenneth Harris just before her accession to power that: 'It must be a conviction government. As Prime Minister I could not waste time having any internal arguments.'[5]

The Napoleonic quote figured strongly in the first set of 'photographs' as I laid them out at the London School of Economics in December 1997 in the course of delivering the Leonard Schapiro Lecture for the journal *Government and Opposition*.[6] At the outset, I declared an intellectual interest in that lecture. I had been worried since before the election about the likely nature of a Blair government and had produced what one might call an anticipatory critique of it in a Radio 4 *Analysis* discussion with, among others, Donald Dewar and William Hague, six days before the election. 'You have a commanding figure in Mr Blair', I had solemnly intoned in my best 'British constitution voice'. 'It's going to be a command premiership. I just hope there's a bit of freedom of information and democracy in the Cabinet.'[7]

Eight months later I wondered before the *Government and Opposition* audience whether my concern had proved justified. In the main, I concluded that it had. I sketched in the Prime Minister's downgrading of the full Cabinet meetings, a phenomenon which his pre-Cabinet sessions (first with his deputy John Prescott, then at the so-called 'Big Four' meetings that followed once Robin Cook and Gordon Brown had joined them) did little to mitigate.

Apart from the swathe of constitutional reform business over which the Lord Chancellor, Lord Irvine, presided, it was difficult to see anything like the standard Cabinet committee machine in operation. Economic policy was very much kept to the Government's inner core of the Blair/Brown axis. No.10, under Blair the most presentation-conscious Downing Street ever, kept a tight grip on image (and ensured that image was a potent ingredient in policy-making from its very earliest stages). The then-still-new Strategic Communications Unit in No.10 was but an institutional reflection of a reality that had been powerfully present from the very beginning.

I also adduced primary and written evidence in support of the 'command premiership' thesis. The first piece arrived courtesy of the *Daily Mail* almost exactly a month after Labour won power. It took the form of a leaked Prime Minister's Personal Minute on 'Press Handling'. 'An interesting idea injected into the media,' Blair informed his colleagues, 'will be taken as a statement of Government policy. All new ideas or statements of this sort must be cleared with No.10.'[8]

Confirmation of this particular manifestation of the Napoleonic came the following month when the *Ministerial Code*, Blair's update of the Cabinet rulebook *Questions of Procedure for Ministers*, developed since 1945 by his ten predecessors, was published.[9] Its paragraph 88 has become the sacred text for those who disapprove of over-mighty prime ministers hijacking what is supposed to be a collegiate arrangement (not a feudal system which is something very different) underpinning central government. It reads:

'In order to ensure the effective presentation of Government policy, all major interviews and media appearances, both print and broadcast, should be agreed with the No.10 Press Office before any commitments are entered into. The policy content of all major speeches, press releases and new policy initiatives should be cleared in good time with the No.10 Private Office; the timing and form of announcements should be cleared with the No.10 Press Office. Each department should keep a record of media contacts by both Ministers and officials.'[10]

This paragraph led that most careful of commentators, Peter Riddell, to exclaim at the time: 'Goodbye Cabinet Government. Welcome the Blair Presidency.'[11]

Sir Bernard Ingham, Thatcher's fabled Press Secretary, observed later of his Blairite equivalent, Alistair Campbell: 'The purpose of the Press Secretary is to get into the Prime Minister's mind, under the Prime Minister's skin, and to be able to act as his or her interpreter – *alter ego* to a degree. But I think this lot believe the impossible is achievable – the co-ordination of the presentation of the work of this Government – because ministers have minds of their own. They all have their own spin-doctors and special advisers.'[12]

Even as an ex-political correspondent and Whitehall watcher, I constantly find it difficult to appreciate fully this aspect of the Blair style. For example, early in 1998 as the possibility of a second Gulf War loomed, I made discreet inquiries to see if the Major 'War Cabinet' of 1991 would be the model for a 1998 version should the need arise. I was told it was, but there was now an extra dimension built into the planning. 'What?' I inquired. 'Surely you can guess with New Labour?', came the reply. 'There'll be a shadow committee solely devoted to presentation.'[13]

What did I conclude from my aerial reconnaissance displayed at the LSE last December? That though it was plain Tony Blair was operating a 'variable geometry approach to governance' (I stressed the potentially pluralist influence of the 'task forces', for example), there was plentiful *prima facie* evidence that a command model had been installed in No.10 on 2 May 1997, which was still in the process of refinement and development.[14]

I ended up with one of my Walter Bagehot impressions by declaring that: 'The only kind of Cabinet government Mr Blair has seen at close hand is his own version. Those who have had close encounters with past Prime Ministers *do* think he is taking a highly prime-ministerial approach towards administration. The forms of Cabinet government may still be apparent, the substance is not. And the sooner his Cabinet ministers, the Downing Street collective as a whole, put that right the better it will be for the government and for the country.'[15]

The lecture produced some intriguing refinements provided by people very close to the new inner core yet capable of applying the kind of perspective that only a long association with the 'core executive' (a concept which most insiders do not recognise and a phrase they cannot abide, by the way) can provide.

Before I turn to that, may I briefly outline my second attempt at photography in flight? It took place in the spring of 1998 and concentrated upon the constitution, the remaking of which already distinguishes the Blair government from any of its predecessors. Yet the rolling transformation of the British constitution features surprisingly seldom in most treatments of events since May 1997. For example, in the most toe-curling public example of prime ministerialism since he took office – Blair's launch of the first annual report of the government, before assorted ministers, civil servants and the media assembled on the Downing Street lawn on 30 July 1998[16] – the document to which he was speaking devoted a third of a page to constitutional reform (much of which had to do with Northern Ireland – an area, incidentally, where a high degree of prime ministerialism is necessary and justified). Over a full page went on his misty notion of a 'Third Way' (or 'Our Values', as he described it), a page-and-a-half on the economy and over half a page on welfare reform.[17]

In the Lloyds TSB Lecture in Glasgow at the end of April 1998, I marvelled at the width of the constitutional reforms, worried about the lack of interest in them on the part of the wider political nation and inside the Cabinet Room, regretted there was no overall strategy for or description of this new, unprecedented constitutional settlement and speculated on the degree to which, once the process is developed and implemented, we will have shifted from an informal, back-of-the-envelope constitution to a more formal, increasingly written one.[18] In passing, I quoted a well-placed Whitehall insider to the effect that: 'Most of the senior ministers involved in constitutional reform either don't believe in it, aren't interested in it or don't understand it.'[19] Another insider told me it was just as well ministers had decided from the outset against issuing a declaratory white paper linking and describing the whole programme of constitutional change as they could have recoiled from the prospect had they appreciated it in the round.[20]

Now, in late 1998, there *are* signs of just such a recoiling. Freedom of information legislation will not be in the legislative programme for the coming session of Parliament.[21] Ministerial responsibility for it shifted from the bullish Cabinet Office to the bearish Home Office when David Clark was removed from the Chancellorship of the Duchy of Lancaster in the July reshuffle (though the Lord Chancellor will remain in the chair of the CRP (FOI) Cabinet Committee overseeing the policy).[22] The Home Secretary and his officials have never been happy with the 'substantial harm' test[23] to be applied to disclosure requests as outlined in the December 1997 white paper, *Your Right to Know*.[24] And, most significant of all, the Prime Minister's spokesman warned of the dangers of 'constitutional overload' which Blair was determined to avoid when the Cabinet broke up after its Chequers 'away day' on 10 September.[25] Taken together, the Government's constitutional changes on the devolution and human rights fronts already amount by UK standards to change on a Napoleonic scale but, paradoxically, most ministers remain reluctant, cautious and apologetic, if not silent, Bonapartists, on constitutional matters at least.

But here we must confront the greatest paradox of all which lies at the heart of the Blair style of government. Never have we experienced a government engaged in such a deliberate process of

constitutional decentralisation through substantial devolution to
Scotland, a lesser tranche to Wales, a shift from a duties polity to
a rights culture with incorporation of the European Convention
on Human Rights into UK domestic law (the magnitude and, for
the executive-minded, inconvenience of which few ministers have
begun to appreciate, though their civil servants have[26]) with a
version of freedom of information and – possibly – proportional
representation for Westminster still to come. Yet never – not even
under late Thatcher when, as Nigel Lawson put it recently, 'She
had become a mythic figure and had begun to believe her own
myth'[27] – have we seen such a centralisation of power around the
incumbent of No.10.

Paddy Ashdown, who sits regularly with the Prime Minister on
the Government's Joint Consultative Cabinet Committee with the
Liberal Democrats on matters of mutual (and so far, exclusively
constitutional) interest, put it recently: 'The most interesting
thing about this Government is the mismatch between the
personalities of the Prime Minister and of his Government. The
former is open, pluralist, democratic, modernising, but the
character of the Government is control freak.'[28] I'm with Thatcher
rather than Ashdown on this one. In spring 1998, she found
herself at a banquet in Buckingham Palace separated from the
Queen and Blair only by a vast bowl of flowers. 'I'm worried
about that young man', she confided to her neighbour, a former
colleague. 'He's getting awfully bossy', said the warrior queen (as
opposed to the real one) without a trace of self-irony. The ex-
Conservative minister nearly fell off his chair.[29] Mind you, there
is a touch of the paradoxical about Lady Thatcher here, too. She
has been letting it be known of late that she regards the shift of
power on interest rates to the Bank of England's Monetary Policy
Committee as 'wimpish' on the grounds that she and her
Chancellors of the Exchequer were tough enough to take the hard
decisions themselves.[30]

The keys to the Blair paradox are firstly, I suspect, a matter of
temperament. We have in the Prime Minister a politician

impatient of tradition whether he finds it in his party, the Labour movement (a term I can rarely recall him using as PM – it seems to me he has borrowed Labour rather than owning it) or in Whitehall. As one permanent secretary put it, it became plain that 'the new Government did not want the old Cabinet system perhaps not even the Cabinet itself. The PM didn't see why you needed an elaborate and slow system of decision taking.'[31] Secondly, it is a matter of what the French call *mentalité*. As Peter Riddell put it: 'Mr Blair thinks politically, not constitutionally. He is sensitive to moods, not structures.'[32] Blair expressed this approach himself in his Fabian pamphlet *The Third Way* when he wrote of his notion of 'permanent revisionism' which he defined as 'a continual search for better means to meet our goals ...'[33]

So, has anything happened to retouch the colours of the picture I painted in the Schapiro Lecture in December 1997? The frame stays the same but more detail and background can now be filled in. Let me explain. Firstly, a number of very well placed inside sources who read my text kindly helped me with this.

For example, I was given a vivid impression of those policy areas where Blair was a 'hands-on and detail-oriented Prime Minister' (as opposed to a premier-for-the-big-picture). 'On Northern Ireland, Europe, welfare reform, education, devolution, health and the New Deal', my informant continued, 'he remains focused on what matters ... and seeks to communicate them as part of an overall strategic approach to the modernisation of Britain. So he is both big picture and detail.'[34] This is a January 1998 snapshot taken by the innermost core and interpreted by them.

This self-view is especially important as, compared to most previous premierships, *permanent* (as opposed to temporary) Whitehall is not always best placed to know what goes on in the Prime Minister's Room even at foreseeable sessions such as the 'Prescott bilateral' or the 'Big Four' meetings on a Thursday morning. As one of the better positioned of permanent Whitehall put it: 'What the mandarinate got wrong about the transition [from Major to Blair] was the degree to which they [Labour ministers] would carry on as they had behaved in opposition. Usually people put that behind them when they get the car and the red box. Not this lot. They have brought their own people with them and they still work through their familiars.'[35]

'This', he continued, 'is especially true of Blair, Brown and Straw, though not Prescott who is different because he wasn't shadowing Environment or Transport before he came in. He brought relatively few people with him so he has had to work much more through the traditional machine.'[36]

But probably the most interesting comment on my December 1997 picture came from a well-placed Whitehall lifer who suggested I might consider an entirely different geopolitical model when mapping the geography of power around Tony Blair. 'The real core is No.10 and No.11,' he said. And despite the regularly aired tensions between the Blair and Brown camps (and it is chiefly a matter of inter-entourage tension rather than difficulties between Premier and Chancellor themselves), this remains the case as the final determination of the outcomes of the hugely, centrally important Comprehensive Spending Review showed.[37] The CSR was very much a PM–Chancellor, Treasury–No.10 Policy Unit affair with the affected departments getting very little look-in during the crucial last weeks. The Cabinet Office was involved, but not as a big player, and what was then the Cabinet's public expenditure committee, PX, definitely did not figure as the locus of decision taking.[38]

While never losing sight of the near overwhelming importance of that No.10 and No.11 Downing Street axis, my insider–helper suggested that a model of concentric circles fitted the reality much more than a pyramidical, hierarchical arrangement of the kind usually produced when the traditionally collective Cabinet system is depicted. In circle one he placed (this is at the turn of 1997/1998) the Prime Minister, Alistair Campbell, Blair's Chief of Staff, Jonathan Powell, the No.10 Private Office under the Prime Minister's Principal Private Secretary, the career diplomat John

Holmes, and the Downing Street Policy Unit headed by David Miliband. Circle 2 he defined as Circle 1 plus Brown, Prescott, Irvine and the then Minister-without-Portfolio, Peter Mandelson. Circle 3 he drew as 1 and 2 plus Prescott. Circle 4 was 1–3 plus Straw and Cook. Circle 5 was 1–4 'plus everyone else'.[39] This in geometric terms is more a court than a Cabinet structure. On paper it looks like this:

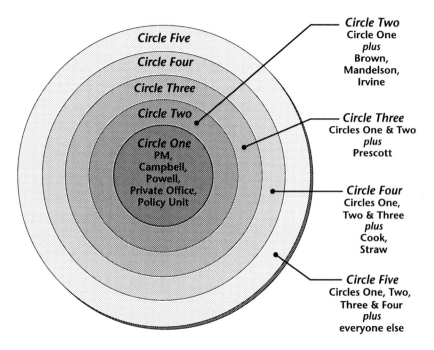

Circle Two
Circle One
plus
Brown,
Mandelson,
Irvine

Circle Three
Circles One & Two
plus
Prescott

Circle Four
Circles One,
Two & Three
plus
Cook,
Straw

Circle Five
Circles One, Two,
Three & Four
plus
everyone else

Circle Five
Circle Four
Circle Three
Circle Two
Circle One
PM,
Campbell,
Powell,
Private Office,
Policy Unit

If one were drawing, Dante-style, the circles of Blair's power structure as it now is, certain difficulties arise with the late 1997/early 1998 model. I have a sense that Straw is now further in and Irvine further out. Straw's receipt of the lead on freedom of information policy confirmed his status as an accomplished and safe pair of hands in the Prime Minister's eyes; Irvine's loss of the chairmanship of the Cabinet's legislation committee (QFL) to the new Leader of the House, Margaret Beckett, does represent a diminution of his power.[40]

Mandelson, as Secretary of State for Trade and Industry, a Cabinet Minister and *departmental* as opposed to a *central* player in his own right, is exceedingly difficult to place. We need more time on that one. Mandelson is always a man of mystery and menace and charm in equal measures. The most interesting question is where to put the new, so-called 'Cabinet Enforcer', Jack Cunningham, who, as the post-reshuffle Chancellor of the Duchy of Lancaster and Minister for the Cabinet Office, has the former portfolios of David Clark and Peter Mandelson rolled-up in his person – plus, if he is to be effective, a bit more.[41]

May I for a moment, keep sight of the 'court' question? Before the general election of 1997, I was concerned that two 'courts' might be in operation if Labour won – a Prime Minister's 'court' and a Chancellor of the Exchequer's 'court'. For it was quite plain from Gordon Brown's pattern of work as Shadow Chancellor that not only did he intend to keep to the Conservatives' planned expenditure ceiling for the first two years of the new administration's life, he was likely also to tie Treasury-shaped policy outcomes to those pockets of public money he was willing to disburse to individual departments.

Given that the No.10–No.11 relationship is in peacetime 'the most important hinge in the whole of the government', as Nigel Lawson put it[42], I sensed the danger of two policy agendas, close-linked but with differences of emphases, emanating uneasily from two of the three 'principal parts of the centre' with the third, the Cabinet Office, unable to do much to reconcile them in the absence of any serious collective machinery for pulling together economic policy as a whole. The Prime Minister's decision not to chair the main Cabinet committee on economic affairs, the first PM since 1964-66 to leave it to another minister, heightened my sense of this.[43]

Have we, in fact, seen the development of such a 'rival court' phenomenon? No, we have not – at least not in the conduct of economic policy – despite a spate of articles on the No.10–No.11 tensions. The Cabinet's Economic Committee, EA, is not the forum where serious or strategic economic policy is shaped. That happens within the very frequent bilateral sessions between Blair and Brown. The handling of the final stage of the Comprehensive Spending Review conformed very much to this existing pattern.

A powerful impression of a Treasury 'court' is created, however, by the Chancellor's temperament and work style. I asked a senior Treasury official recently if Brown had matured somewhat in the sense of taking counsel more widely from the permanent Treasury as opposed to the special advisers, Ed Balls especially, whom he brought into the building with him from Opposition? 'No', he replied. 'He never will. The Chancellor is an anorak. He has the social skills of a whelk.'[44] Though to be fair, relationships between official Treasury and ministerial Treasury have noticeably improved since Sir Andrew Turnbull succeeded Lord Burns as Permanent Secretary during the summer.[45]

Seasoned Whitehall watchers may have noticed that so far, I have said surprisingly little about the third, and usually sturdily indispensable leg of the central tripod of government – the Cabinet Office. Indeed, another figure whom it is difficult to place inside the concentric circles of the Blair 'court' is Sir Richard Wilson who replaced Sir Robin Butler as Secretary of the Cabinet in January 1998. Unlike Sir Robin, who had been in the post for a decade serving both Thatcher and John Major, Richard Wilson was Blair-picked, and high hopes were invested in the first special task set for him by the Prime Minister – a review designed to map out and create that more dynamic centre on the creation of which Blair was set along the lines described by Peter Mandelson and Roger Liddle in their pre-election study, *The Blair Revolution*.[46]

Sir Richard was confronted by what might seem an insoluble dilemma for a man of great experience who is neither feudal nor Napoleonic by temperament but collective; more a servant of the Cabinet as a whole than Prime Minister's 'Whitehall Chief Whip'.[47] (In this he was quite indistinguishable from his predecessor, Sir Robin Butler.[48]) Sir Richard puts it rather differently himself. He describes as 'a key role' for the Cabinet Office that it 'holds the ring'.[49] As he put it to a conference of officials last week, 'the Cabinet Office ought to be available for the Centre to communicate to Departments and for Departments to communicate to the Centre. I want No.10 to feel that they can say to us "What is happening in Department X?" or "I'd like to give them this message". And I'd like Department X to feel that they can say to us "What is No.10 thinking on this issue? Can you help us get this through?"'[50]

Those who know Sir Richard well observed two parallel tracks at work in his first half-year as Cabinet Secretary. It was quite plain, first of all, from the way he worked day-by-day that he would try to bridge the old and the new in a palpable if unobtrusive way. As one close observer put it: 'Richard would almost wait around seeming to be useful. He played it brilliantly and waited. And, bit by bit, as ministers continued doing things without consulting each other, and getting into trouble, he began to offer a brokerage – almost a conciliation – service. He could not have produced these ways of preserving much of the old system while fitting in with the wishes of the new Prime Minister if he hadn't waited.'[51] The review, expected to be swift, was not completed until Maundy Thursday and the Prime Minister did not get round to publishing his thoughts upon it until just before the summer recess. So what exactly were these Wilsonian 'ways' of preserving the old alongside the new?

In essence, this. Sir Richard's solution was, as one close colleague put it, to fashion 'new corporate bricks' from the masonry of the traditional Cabinet system.[52] Old material for new purposes, might be an accurate shorthand for this approach – building a structure that fits the Prime Minister's wishes with bricks that have been used before but rearranged in a different configuration. Stripped to its essentials, the Wilson philosophy is that the Cabinet Office has to provide a service to the collective *through* the Prime Minister who is not only the keeper of the Government's strategy but the Minister for the Civil Service as well. So Wilson serves the PM both as Cabinet Secretary and Head of the Home Civil Service. Jack Cunningham appreciates this duality very well and reckons his clout and authority will rest on his being able to say 'Tony says so' and 'I have taken advice from the Cabinet Secretary and this is what he says ...'[53]

Sir Richard Wilson's perspective removes any need for a Prime Minister's Department or any tampering with the unwritten constitution or the legal position of Secretaries of State. For him, No.10 and the Cabinet Office will always have separate but complementary functions, with the collective functions of the Cabinet Office rooted strongly in departments and the Cabinet and its committees remaining the formal, symbolic centre of decision taking.[54]

So, how have the Prime Minister and the Cabinet Secretary reconciled Bonapartist impulses with the collective practices and mechanics tried and tested since Sir Maurice Hankey and David Lloyd George trod where they are now treading almost 82 years ago? All we have as yet in the public domain is the Prime Minister's parliamentary answer of 28 July 1998 to Gwyneth Dunwoody's request that he make 'a statement on the future of the Cabinet Office.'

The opening section of Blair's reply was pure Sir Richard Wilson in its philosophy: 'The role of the Cabinet Office has traditionally been to help the Prime Minister and the Government as a whole to reach collective decisions on Government policy. Since the election, the three principal parts of the centre – my own office, the Cabinet Office and the Treasury – have worked closely and effectively together, and with other Departments, to take forward the Government's comprehensive and ambitious policy agenda.'[55]

Plainly a deal had been struck between old and new in a very unBonapartist preamble. However, the status quo was not enough. Wilson, Blair told the Commons, had identified weakness in the linkage between centre and periphery; policy formation, implementation and monitoring; Whitehall mechanisms and delivery; forward looks that embraced both difficulty and potential.

All of this the PM's people bundle up under the label of 'joined-up government'[56], the new cross-departmentalism which Blair stressed in his pamphlet *The Third Way*.[57]

The Social Exclusion Unit, a cross-departmental body in the Cabinet Office that brings outsiders and insiders, the centre and the periphery together to tackle the knottiest problems which go into the making of serious deprivation, will be the model for the future here[58] (and Blair first used the 'joined-up-government' phrase when launching the SEU[59]). So will the new Cabinet Committee on Public Services and Public Expenditure, PSX, which will monitor the public service agreements concluded between the Treasury and all departments (except, interestingly enough, No.10 and the Cabinet Office) as part of the Comprehensive Spending Review under which money will only be released by the Treasury if departments stick to their plans.[60] In this new Treasury-periphery arrangement we could well see, as it develops, the manifestation of a Brown policy agenda, unless the Prime Minister ensures it becomes a part of their regular bilateral economic discussions. The idea is that a Cabinet Office moulded around the new style No.10 will work in a complementary rather than a duplicatory fashion alongside the Treasury. We shall see.

For also emerging from the Wilson review is a new Cabinet Office Performance and Innovation Unit (could this be a partial return of the Central Policy Review Staff killed off by Thatcher in 1983 and, if it is, might it not become a challenger to the Treasury's primacy as demonstrated by those public service agreements with departments?) One of the chief purposes of the PIU, as Richard Wilson put it, will be to 'take a limited number of projects' to be decided by the Prime Minister 'in consultation with the secretaries of state concerned.' Teams of insiders and outsiders will then be put together to examine 'the strategic objectives' the PM, his Policy Unit and ministers 'want to reach in five to ten years time'.[61] This has a real CPRS-ish flavour about it.

There is also to be a new Centre for Management and Policy Studies in the Cabinet Office to help create a revived sense of common Whitehall citizenship among senior civil servants while drawing in new thinking from the academic and policy analysis worlds. The Civil Service College will move into its orbit.[62] It should be up and running next spring and looks set to become a resource for much of the public sector.[63] There is, too, to be a fusing of the Civil Service management side and the Cabinet Secretariat slice of the Cabinet Office.[64] The Permanent Secretaries' 'College of Cardinals' is to be retained in the shape of Sir Richard Wilson's Wednesday morning meeting but a smaller Management Board for the Civil Service will be created alongside it, probably consisting of 15 or so heads of the major departments with sub-committees spun out of it.[65] Plainly the feeling is that the Civil Service, and not merely the PM, needs a stronger centre and there seems to have been genuine support for this at the Permanent Secretaries' annual autumn meeting in October.[66]

The Prime Minister's brief, three-page parliamentary answer outlining the new centre was wrapped up by another statement of the constitutionally impeccable – 'The Cabinet Office will continue to report to me as Prime Minister and Minister for the Civil Service. I will continue to account to Parliament for matters of collective Cabinet responsibility; the Minister for the Cabinet Office [Jack Cunningham] will report to Parliament on the management of the Civil Service and allied matters and, in particular, will oversee the major programme of reform I am announcing today.'[67]

All this will need watching – but notice already from that statement how Jack Cunningham has been kept out of the crucial work of the full Cabinet Secretariat, the pitch primers for the Cabinet and its committees, even though his title is 'Minister for the Cabinet Office'. Here Sir Richard Wilson's lines are straight to Blair. Dr Cunningham is a seasoned player but he had been barred from the central policy playing field from day one. This is why placing him in the right concentric circle is difficult. He's in circle two at best; maybe three.

All this make for a wonderfully fluid picture – the stuff of exam papers to come. By next spring, when I'll overfly SW1 once more with the cameras on, some things (like the human side and the power flows of the new centre) will be clearer – as one cynic said, 'We have a soft spot for Jack Cunningham. We've already started digging it.'[68] We are promised more details on the Blair/Wilson settlement in the *Better Government* white paper (expected in early 1999).[69] Though what we really need is for Sir Richard Wilson's Maundy Thursday Minute to the Prime Minister to be published and I have a feeling that we may indeed get an edited version of it before too long.[70]

But I suspect it will be not the foreseeable but the unforeseen – what Harold Macmillan famously called the 'opposition of events'[71] – that will shape the people and the practices at the core of central government by the time I take off next spring. Already ministers are grappling with problems not worked on in Opposition and unforeseen in the manifesto (the finances of Japan and the Far East; everything to do with Russia) and those which the manifesto glossed over (the problems associated with merely touching the composition, let alone the power, of the second chamber; a genuine debate and decision on proportional representation for Westminster elections). And then there are those 72 task forces commissioned in the period of high optimism whose reports will come flooding in as the possibilities appear to narrow.[72]

As a very central and very seasoned member of the *permanent* government put it: 'I believe the form of the Blair government is not going to be apparent for about two years. We are doing a lot of re-engineering in flight. Just think, when did we really know what Mrs T's government would be like? Not until 1981.'[73] I shall be making my overflights for years to come. But one thing I can predict with confidence, the Blair style will remain an issue of fascination and contention, and the tension between Prime Minister and Cabinet will not be resolved. In political life, as Napoleon himself found, there are no permanent victories. And on the Cabinet's Chequers 'away day' on 10 September 1998, every one of them contributed – a first for the Blair premiership.[74] And about time too, though one must not read too much into this little burst of collegiality in Buckinghamshire.

There was reliable information in the autumn of 1998 which indicated that regular Thursday Cabinets were as perfunctory as ever – rarely longer than 30 to 40 minutes in duration. And even this deep into government, though there was a formal Cabinet agenda, the Prime Minster still did not stick to it. Discursive is the word to describe his style. 'The Cabinet minutes', one insider told me at that time, 'are largely a matter of *ex post facto* rationalisation by the Cabinet Secretariat. Cabinet under this Prime Minister,' he concluded, 'has been reduced to a virtual cypher.'[75] I regret to say he is right and it worries me. It does not have to be like that. Collegiate premiers can preside – and have presided – over governments with a strong and sustained sense of direction. As Nye Bevan liked to remark, 'Why gaze in the crystal ball when you can read it in the book.'[76]

It is possible for traditionally-minded observers to apply a kind of false veneration to the bundle of practices that have gone into the making of Cabinet government since the eighteenth century (what the cultural historian, Richard Weight, has called in another context 'making the everyday sacramental'[77]). But attention to the *longue durée* of British governance does induce a sense of and respect for the importance of being collective, both as a safeguard against overmightiness at the top and as an aid to careful, effective and durable policy making. Command models, Napoleonic or otherwise, have a habit of ending in tears. The temptation to install and operate them is best resisted.

Notes

1 House of Commons, *Official Report*, 28 July 1998.

2 Private information.

3 Address by Tony Blair to the Newspaper Society, London, 10 March 1997.

4 *The Matrix of Power*, BBC Radio 4, 10 September 1998.

5 *The Observer*, 25 February 1979.

6 Peter Hennessy, 'The Blair style of government: an historical perspective and an interim audit', *Government and Opposition*, Vol 33, No 1, Winter 1998, pp. 3-20.

7 *Analysis*, BBC Radio 4, 24 April 1997.

8 Sonia Purnell, 'Cabinet big guns gagged by Blair', *Daily Mail*, 2 June 1997.

9 A definitive study of the development of *Questions of Procedure for Ministers* will be published in 1999 by Amy Baker in her *Prime Ministers and the Rulebook*.

10 *Ministerial Code: A Code of Conduct and Guidance on Procedures for Ministers*, (Cabinet Office, July 1997), p.30.

11 Peter Riddell, 'Tories should focus on what really matters', *The Times*, 1 August 1998.

12 Sir Bernard was speaking on *The Matrix of Power*, 10 September 1998.

13 Private information.

14 Hennessy, 'The Blair Style of Government', op.cit., pp. 15-16.

15 Ibid. p. 20.

16 Sue Cameron, 'Whitehall grovels to Millbank', *The Times*, 18 August 1998.

17 Speech by Tony Blair, 10 Downing Street, 30 July 1998.

18 Peter Hennessy, 'Re-engineering the state in flight: a year in the life of the British constitution, April 1997-April 1998', delivered at the Burrell Collection, Glasgow on 30 April 1998 and published by the Lloyds TSB Group plc in July 1988.

19 Ibid p. 9.

20 Ibid.

21 Andrew Parker, 'Freedom of information bill to be postponed', *Financial Times*, 29 September 1998.

22 *Ministerial Committees of the Cabinet* (Cabinet Office, October 1998).

23 Private information.

24 *Your Right to Know: Freedom of Information*, Cm 3813 (Cabinet Office/Office of Public Service, December 1997), p. 16.

25 Andrew Grice, 'Blair to delay electoral reform', *The Independent*, 11 September 1998.

26 Private information.

27 Lord Lawson was speaking on *In The Psychiatrist's Chair*, BBC Radio 4, 25 September 1998.

28 Peter Riddell and Roland Watson, 'Ashdown prepares to claim PR price', *The Times*, 18 September 1998.

29 Private information.

30 Private information.

31 Private information.

32 Peter Riddell, 'Hard heads, not soft hearts', *The Times*, 31 August 1998.

33 Tony Blair, *The Third Way: New Politics for the New Century*, Fabian Pamphlet 588 (Fabian Society, 1998), p. 4.

34 Private information.

35 Private information.

36 Private information.

37 The outcome of the Comprehensive Spending Review was published in July 1998 as *Modern Public Services for Britain: Investing in Reform*, Cm 4011 (HM Treasury, July 1998). For perhaps the most bravura press example of the 'neighbours at war' story see Seumas Milne, 'Division of labour', *The Guardian*, 1 July 1998.

38 Private information.

39 Private information.

40 *Ministerial Committees of the Cabinet* (Cabinet Office, October 1998).

41 Patrick Wintour, 'Blair's July plot for peace', *The Observer*, 2 August 1998; Valerie Elliott, 'Blair creates crisis centre at Cabinet Office', *The Times*, 29 July 1998.

42 Lord Lawson, *In The Psychiatrist's Chair*.

43 *Ministerial Committees of the Cabinet* (Cabinet Office, June 1997). Gordon Brown chairs the EA committee as it is known.

44 Private information.

45 Private information.

46 Peter Mandelson and Roger Liddle, *The Blair Revolution: Can New Labour Deliver?* (Faber, 1996), pp. 232-46.

47 Private information.

48 Private information.

49 Sir Richard Wilson, 'Modernising central government: the role of the senior civil service', speech to senior civil servants, London, 13 October 1998.

50 Ibid.

51 Private information.

52 Private information.

53 Elliott, 'Blair creates crisis centre at Cabinet Office.' op.cit.

54 Private information.

55 House of Commons, *Official Report*, 28 July 1998.

56 A phrase one hears constantly and which is in danger of becoming a piece of linguistic litter.

57 Blair, *The Third Way*, op.cit., p. 16.

58 Ibid.

59 Tony Blair, civil service conference speech, 13 October 1998.

60 House of Commons, *Official Report*, 14 July 1998, and *Ministerial Committees of the Cabinet* (Cabinet Office, October 1998).

61 Wilson, 'Modernising central government' op.cit.

62 House of Commons, *Official Report*, 28 July 1998.

63 Private information.

64 House of Commons, *Official Report*, 28 July 1998.

65 Private information.

66 Private information.

67 House of Commons, *Official Report*, 28 July 1998.

68 Private information.

69 House of Commons, *Official Report*, 28 July 1998 and private information.

70 Private information.

71 See Peter Hennessy, *The Hidden Wiring: Unearthing the British Constitution* (Gollancz, 1995), p. 165.

72 Conversation with Sir Len Peach, the Commissioner for Public Appointments (who has to keep a tally of such things), 29 July 1998.

73 Private information.

74 Private information.

75 Private information.

76 This is the colloquial version that has echoed down the corridors of political memory. What Bevan actually said to Robert Boothby during a Westminster debate in 1949 was: 'Why read the crystal when he can read the book?' House of Commons, *Official Report*, 29 September 1949.

77 Conversation with Dr Richard Weight, the Oval Cricket Ground, 29 August 1998.